What Do You Think?

Can Earth Support Our Growing Population?

Kate Shuster

Heinemann Library
Chicago, Illinois

Editorial: Andrew Farrow and Rebecca Vickers
Design: Philippa Jenkins
Picture Research: Melissa Allison and Ruth Blair
Production: Alison Parsons

Originated by Heinemann Library
Printed and bound in China

13 12 11 10 09
10 9 8 7 6 5 4 3 2 1

Library of Congress Cataloging-in-Publication Data
Shuster, Kate, 1974-
    Can earth support our growing population? / Kate Shuster.
        p. cm. -- (What do you think?)
    Includes bibliographical references and index.
    ISBN 978-1-4329-1673-2 (hc)
    1. Population. 2. Consumption (Economics) I. Title.
    HB871.S557 2008
    363.9'1--dc22
                                              2008014659

Acknowledgments
The author and publishers are grateful to the following for permission to reproduce copyright material: © Alamy/Jenny Matthews p. **45**; ©Biosphoto/Gunther Michel/Still Pictures p. **18**; © Copyright 2006 SASI Group (University of Sheffield) and Mark Newman (University of Michigan) www.worldmapper.org pp. **13**, **14**; © Corbis pp. **21**, **23**, /Bettmann **40**, /Colin Garratt Milepost 92½ **34**, /Karen Kasmauski **10**, **36**, /Liba Taylor **38**, /Louise Gubb **43**, /Reg Charity **9**; © Getty Images/ PhotoDisc pp. **30**, **44**; © NASA/Goddard Space Flight Center Scientific Visualization Studio p. **32**; © Jeff Parker, *Florida Today* p. **49**; © PhotoEdit/Rhoda Sidney p. **46**; © Rex Features/Alisdair Macdonald p. **4**; © Science Photo Library p. **12**, /Mauro Fermariello **24**; © Kate Shuster p. **51**.

Cover photograph reproduced with permission of © Rex Features and © Getty Images/Photodisc.

The publishers would like to thank Dr. Michael Richards for his assistance in the preparation of this book.

Every effort has been made to contact copyright holders of any material reproduced in this book. Any omissions will be rectified in subsequent printings if notice is given to the publisher.

Disclaimer
All the Internet addresses (URLs) given in this book were valid at the time of going to press. However, due to the dynamic nature of the Internet, some addresses may have changed, or sites may have changed or ceased to exist since publication. While the author and publishers regret any inconvenience this may cause readers, no responsibility for any such changes can be accepted by either the author or the publishers.

Table of Contents

Some words are shown in bold, **like this**. You can find out what they mean by looking in the Glossary.

> *How many is too many?*

As cities and nations become more crowded, space and resources like food, water, and fuel may become increasingly scarce. Does a larger population necessarily mean a lower standard of living? Are there enough resources to go around?

Our Growing Population?

The world's population has more than doubled since 1950, and it continues to grow. Some people think our population will double again in fifty more years. But Earth remains the same size. Some people think that our planet is too small and too limited to continue to support an ever-increasing number of people. Other people think that population growth won't be a problem, as long as we change the way we share Earth's **resources**.

In this book, you'll explore the causes and consequences of the population boom. You'll learn why population is increasing, and why some people think this is a challenge. You'll examine different areas of the world where population growth is creating difficulties and opportunities. Along the way, you will be asked to think critically about the evidence and ideas being presented, evaluating different perspectives on the related issues of population and resource distribution.

Finally, you'll be asked to form your own opinion about the book's title question: Can Earth support our growing population?

Understanding population growth

When we refer to the number of individuals in an area or nation, we call them a population. Your school, city, nation, and planet, has a population. It may have a relatively stable, or unchanging, population. For example, schools often set limits on how many students can enroll. Cities might only have a fixed amount of housing, limiting the number of people who can live there. Most places have populations that change over time. We call these dynamic populations. The number of people in a place may grow if more people move in or out, if people live longer or get sick, or if more babies are born. Populations have growth rates, which express the degree of change over time. In any given year, the rate of growth can be expressed as births minus deaths divided by the total population. So, if Earth had 100 residents, and 20 were born while 10 died, the population's growth rate would be .10, or 10 percent. Growth rates are normally expressed as percentages or fractions relative to the total population.

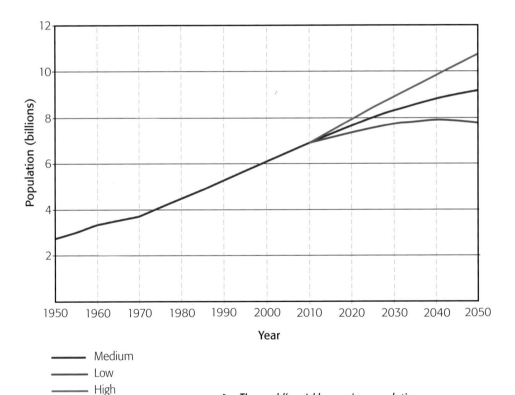

Medium
Low
High

> *The world's quickly growing population*

This graph shows what the world population might be by 2050. The different estimates represent different fertility rates—in other words, if people are having more babies (higher fertility), the population will grow more.

Exponential growth

Earth's population is growing quickly. This is because population growth occurs **exponentially**. In math, an exponent expresses a multiplier effect where a number is multiplied by itself. So 2^2 is two to the second power, or two times two. 2^3 is two to the third power, or two times two times two. Populations increase exponentially because every two adults can produce more children, who in turn can produce more children.

To visualize this process, imagine a family tree. At the top are two people—perhaps your great-great grandparents. Beneath them are their children—your grandparents and great-aunts and uncles. At each point in the family tree, more branches are created. As long as people in the family keep having children, the family will get larger with each generation.

✔ Population change: fertility and mortality

Fertility has to do with how many babies a society produces. If a couple has only one baby, they are said to be below the **replacement fertility rate** for the population. The couple is not replacing their own number in the population. Over time, if a country has fewer children than adults, the population of that country will shrink as adults die off, and there are fewer children to replace them. On the other hand, if more children are born than adults, a country will exceed its replacement rate and the population will increase. Factors that can affect fertility rates include poverty, security, birth control, and religion. Different countries have different fertility rates.

Of course, not all babies survive to adulthood, and not all people live long lives. Mortality affects population size, because if more people die than are born, a country's population will decrease. Several factors may affect **mortality rates** including infant mortality (how many people die as babies), disease rates, or healthcare resources.

If countries have good healthcare systems, people will live longer, leading to reduced mortality rates. Poverty, wars, and disease **epidemics** may increase death rates, reducing populations overall, even if many babies are being born. Different countries also have different mortality rates.

180,000 a day

If a population is growing at five percent per year, the population size will generally double in 14 years. Currently, Earth's population is growing at a rate just over one percent. But with 6.6 billion people, this means that 66 million people are added each year. Every day, on average, more than 180,000 people are born all around the world. While the world's growth rate is projected to go down to less than half a percent per year, that's still adding a lot of people every year.

Resources and consumption

In itself, population growth is not necessarily a bad thing. You might live in a rural area where more people could be helpful to produce more crops, run more businesses, or teach different subjects in school. Or it might be a good idea to have more people in your community to pay more taxes. But people need things—they need roads, and schools, and food. And when there are more people around, they need more of those things. We call those things resources. A resource might be anything from water to electricity. When we **consume** resources, we use them up. Some resources are **renewable resources**. This means that we can make them again—like plants, which can be grown again, or solar power, which we don't use up. Other resources are nonrenewable. This means that once we use them, they're gone. Coal is an example of a nonrenewable resource. There is only so much coal in the ground to mine, and we can't make more.

One of the biggest questions, then, about Earth's growing population is the relationship between population and resources. Are there enough resources to go around? Will an increased population cause resource shortages, or are shortages caused by other factors, such as some people consuming more than their share of the available resources? Do we really need to worry about population growth at all?

Making arguments about population growth

This book encourages you to make an informed opinion about whether or not Earth can sustain its growing population. In order to do so, you're going to have to consider the arguments presented on different sides of different issues. These opinions should be well supported. Expressing your opinion as an argument in favor of a particular position means that you need to include reasoning and evidence when advancing an idea. This is the **A–R–E** format for expressing an opinion, where an argument includes an **a**ssertion, **r**easoning, and **e**vidence.

Reasoning is the "because" part of an argument. It provides the logic for your position, showing why it is more likely to be true than false. Let's say that your opinion about population growth is that it will be an increasing problem. By itself, that statement doesn't have any support. Adding reasoning will make it more persuasive:

- *Population growth is a problem, because there is not enough water to go around for an increased number of people.*

The "because" statement offers support for your initial idea. But reasoning isn't enough. You should also try to have evidence for your arguments. Evidence is facts, examples, or other support for your reasoning. With the example above, you might add support this way:

- *Population growth is a problem, because there is not enough water to go around for an increased number of people. Already, around 1.4 billion people live in areas where there are water shortages. More people will make this situation worse.*

Including reasoning and evidence as part of your arguments, whether you express them in a speech, in conversation with friends, or in a written essay, will always make your opinions more powerful and harder to knock down.

> *We are all consumers*

Everybody consumes resources every day, from the food you eat to the electricity you use. This hamburger may look tasty. But it takes seven pounds (3 kg) of grain to produce one pound (0.45 kg) of beef. Is this a good use of grain?

> *More people than resources?*

In many parts of the world, resources are already stretched
to the breaking point. Our expanding population may be
bumping up against the limited ability of environments
to provide the resources to sustain humans in a way that
promotes their healthy development.

Are There Limits To Growth?

Sometime in 2012, the world's seven-billionth resident will be born. What kind of life she will have is likely to depend very much on where she is born. If she is lucky enough to be born in one of the world's wealthier countries, she will probably survive childhood and live to have children of her own. During her life, she will have access to plenty of food and water as well as medical care. She is likely to be able to go to school and learn to read and write.

However, it's much more likely that the seven-billionth child will be born into poverty. Like about 60 percent of the world's population, she will probably live in Asia. If she survives into adulthood, she will have a one in three chance of dying or suffering disabilities caused by hunger or poor nutrition. If she is born into poverty, Number Seven Billion will probably never go to school. Our lot in life depends very much on where we are born.

As more people are born, Earth's resources will be stretched even further. Some people believe that this means fewer resources will be available for the seven-billionth child, and even fewer in time for the eight-billionth.

How we're growing

The study of populations and their characteristics is called **demography**. Demographers use statistics to measure the changes in populations over time. They usually examine numbers like birth rates, death rates, average fertility rates (numbers of births per woman), infant mortality rates, and life expectancy (how long someone usually lives). When demographers study specific populations, such as the population of a city, nation, or region, they also take into account how many people move into the region (immigration) as well as how many people move out (emigration).

While demography can tell us about how many people are on Earth and where they live, it can't tell us much about their **standard of living**. The term "standard of living" refers to the kinds and amounts of goods and services that are available to people, and how those goods and services are shared within a population. People with a relatively high standard of living generally have plenty of access to basic needs like food and water, as well as other goods like cars, houses, and clothing. People with a low standard of living are usually poor, without reliable access to goods and services. The average standard of living in a country tells us something about the material wealth of its citizens. But it is definitely possible to live in a poor country and be very rich, or to live in a rich country and be very poor.

> Thomas Malthus (1766-1834)

Concerns about Earth's growing population and its effect on strained natural resources are nothing new. In 1798, Englishman Thomas Robert Malthus wrote his influential *Essay on the Principle of Population*. In this book, he argued that because population tends to increase faster than resource availability, there were likely to be resource shortages. When these shortages occurred, he argued, there would likely be famines or other catastrophic events.

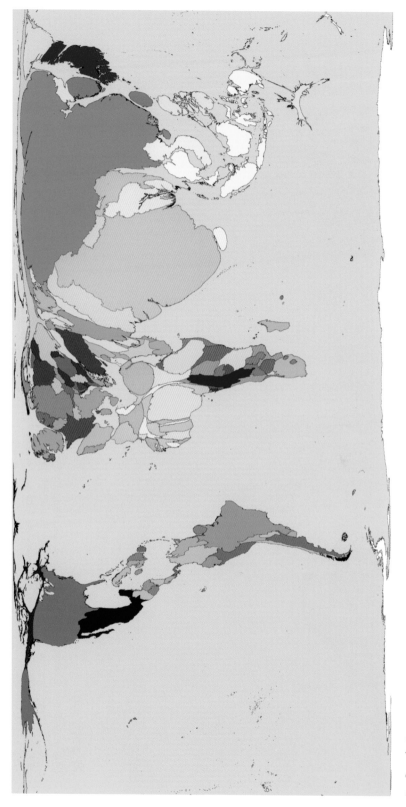

Population map

This map of the world shows countries sized by population, so countries with larger populations are shown proportionately larger than countries with smaller populations. Conventional maps represent country size by land area rather than population size. For the best interpretation of this map, find a conventional map and view the two maps side by side. Which countries are larger on the population map than on the land-size map? Which are smaller? Which continents are the biggest, by population? Which are the smallest? Are there any countries that are bigger or smaller on the population map than you expected?

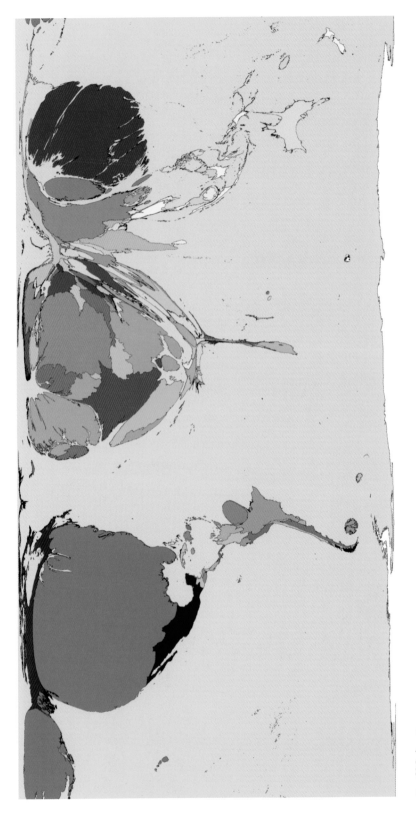

> *GDP density map*

This map shows countries sized by their Gross Domestic Product (GDP). Gross Domestic Product is the total value of all the goods and services produced within a country during a period of time—in this case, within a year. GDP is one way of measuring the total value of a country's economy and the wealth of its residents. Compare this map to the population map. Are the most populated countries also the richest countries? How about the least populated countries?

✔ Mean, median, mode

When people are describing general trends for large numbers of people, they often talk about what the average person does rather than describe what each individual does. For example, if you wanted to talk about how students at your school did on a science test, it would be pretty time consuming to name each student and describe their grade. Instead, you might choose to report the **average** of their grades. This statistic is also called the **mean**. For the science example, you would simply add up all students' grades and divide them by the number of students. This will tell you the average test grade. While the mean grade tells you what you'd expect the average person to receive, it doesn't tell you anything about how the grades are distributed. Let's say that you have a mean score of five out of ten. That could indicate that all students got five questions right. As a teacher, you would need to focus your attention on all the students to make sure they learned more material. But a mean of five could indicate that half of the students got perfect scores and half got no questions right. If this is the case, you'll need to focus on those students who know nothing.

It's good to know the mean, but sometimes you also need to know the **median** score. The median of a list is the middle number, with the same number of items above the median as below it. If you know the median test scores, you know more about how the scores are distributed.

Another way to measure distribution is by looking at the **mode** of a set of numbers. The mode is the number that occurs most frequently. It is not necessarily the same as the mean. Let's say that in your science test experiment, eight students scored a four while two scored a ten. The mean score would be 5.2. This makes it seem like most students got half the questions right. But the mode score is four, so actually most students did not pass the test.

Demographic transitions

Considering the standard of living of a country helps us to understand why different places grow in different ways, at different rates. As countries become wealthier, they tend to grow more slowly or even experience negative population growth. Countries like Japan and Germany actually have shrinking populations. This is, in part, because people live longer in wealthier countries—they have more access to health care and better diets. Also, people who live in wealthier countries tend to have fewer children. There are many competing explanations for this. Some people say that poorer people have more children because they know that fewer children will live to see adulthood. Others say that in poor societies, it is important for families to have more children so that they can support the family through their labor and financial contributions.

Finally, some say that a lack of financial and educational opportunities for women in poor countries means less access to **family planning** and more fertility.

As countries become more industrialized and mean wealth increases, they experience what demographers call a **demographic transition**. A demographic transition happens when the **fertility rate** declines more quickly than the death rate, so that the numbers of older people in a society are increasing more quickly than the numbers of younger people. Most of the world's wealthier countries are already in a demographic transition, with slower or negative population growth.

Disappearing Water

Taskupru, Turkey Arif Karaoglu recalls the days when Lake Aksehir lapped at the foot of the village mosque and residents had to build high walls to protect their homes from flooding. Now, when he looks out across the landscape, he sees only a vast, sandy plateau. Until recently, a body of water three times the size of Washington, D.C. filled the plain. "Dust," laments Mr. Karaoglu, who moved to the village in 1942. "There's nothing but dust."

Dubbed the country's grain warehouse, central Turkey's Konya plain has long been known for its beautiful lakes and vast fields, which produce 10 percent of Turkey's agricultural yield. But both are now threatened by a severe water shortage that dramatically illustrates a broader regional crisis.

Across the Mediterranean, water is being pumped out of the earth at an unsustainable pace. In Italy's Milan region, groundwater levels have fallen by more than 80 feet over the past 80 years. So much water has been pumped from the Jeffara **aquifer** in Libya that even if all withdrawals stopped, it would take 75 years for the aquifer to return to its original level, estimates a 2005 report by the Blue Plan— a United Nations program on development and the environment in the Mediterranean.

[From an article by Nicole Itano in the *Christian Science Monitor* http://www.csmonitor.com/2008/0115/p01s04-woeu.html]

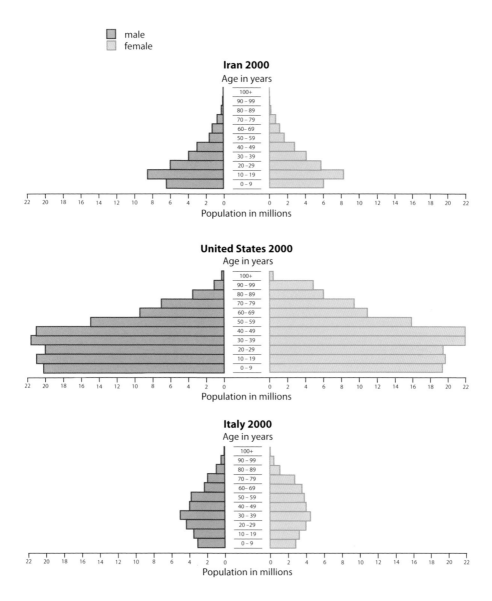

male
female

Iran 2000
Age in years

Population in millions

United States 2000
Age in years

Population in millions

Italy 2000
Age in years

Population in millions

> *Population pyramids*

These charts show a different way to represent population. Sometimes called population pyramids, they illustrate the number of people in a country's population that are of different ages, organized by gender. These three "pyramids" show three countries at different stages of their "demographic transition." Iran is experiencing rapid growth, as most of its residents are young. The United States is experiencing moderate growth. On the pyramid, this is shown by wider bands at the bottom. The bottom pyramid, Italy, is experiencing negative growth.

> Pressure on land

As human populations grow, they need more goods and services. This has meant increasing consumption of both natural and human-produced resources. For example, **deforestation** is increasing as populations grow, especially in poor countries where people seek agricultural land, living space, and income in previously forested areas.

A Consuming Problem

The number of people that can live on Earth may be determined by its "**carrying capacity**." Every **ecosystem** has a carrying capacity. This is the population size it can support with available resources without a significant negative impact on the organisms or the environment. Researchers in biology often grow bacteria in petri dishes, which are small containers that contain nutrient-rich gels. These dishes foster the growth of bacterial colonies, but can only support as many bacteria as there is food and space.

Once food and space run out, the population of bacteria will decline as organisms starve. The carrying capacity has been surpassed, and the dish can no longer sustain a growing population. But Earth's ecosystem is much more complex than a petri dish. Nobody knows for sure if the planet has a carrying capacity, or what that capacity might be. This is because, in part, the amount of resources each person uses varies.

Even though there are a finite number of resources available for human consumption, these resources could be expanded or distributed differently to ensure everyone has access to food, water, and other essentials.

Causes and effects

Everything has at least one cause, just like everything has effects. In human society, just like in the natural world, these causes and effects are usually complex. As an example, consider what you had for lunch today. What caused you to eat that meal? Of course, you ate because you were hungry. But let's say you had pizza for lunch. Why pizza? What chain of events caused pizza to be your lunch? One explanation might be that pizza was cheaper than other items, so it made more financial sense to buy it. Or maybe pizza is your usual lunch, so you went with the familiar option. A third explanation is that you don't usually have pizza, and so you wanted to try it. Leaving alone the immediate decision of "pizza or not," you might also consider the historical circumstances that caused pizza—rather than sushi or curried eggplant or deep-fried grasshoppers—to be served for lunch.

The foods that we eat are markers of cultural exchange and **globalization**, or the global relationships between cultures that are made possible through the movement of people, goods, and ideas. Pizza may not be a food that is native to your part of the world, but it found its way to your lunch table through global exchanges with Italy. In a sense, these exchanges also caused your lunch choice.

For historical events, causality can be hard to pin down. You may have studied the Roman Empire in school. Even well-respected scholars disagree about the reasons why this empire fell. Some say that barbarian invasions caused the fall, while others blame government corruption. One might be the immediate, or **proximate cause**. That's the event that immediately triggers something, like your hunger causing you to eat. The **ultimate cause** is the underlying trigger. So, in the case of the Roman Empire, we might say that invasions were the proximate, or immediate, cause of the fall. But corruption and economic decline caused the people of Rome to welcome, or be unable to resist, the invaders. This might be the ultimate, or underlying cause.

Cause and effect is complicated in the natural world as well. In an ecosystem, animals and plants coexist in relationships that are intertwined and interdependent. When we say that living creatures are interdependent, we mean that they depend on each other to thrive. For example, wolves are dependent on the animals they eat in order to survive as a community. But those animals (like deer) are also dependent on wolves. If there are no wolves to keep down the deer population, it may grow until it strains the carrying capacity of the ecosystem.

> *Passing the frog test*

Species such as this tree frog may seem insignificant and small, but they can be very important to the healthy life of an ecosystem. Frogs control insect populations and are themselves important as a source of food for other animals. Because frogs are very sensitive to changes in the environment, such as increased water pollution, they are often used as an indicator of the health of an ecosystem. If frogs are disappearing, researchers often suspect something is wrong with the ecosystem—not because the frogs are causing it, but because the disappearing frogs are a sign of some other problem.

In ecosystems with hundreds of species of animals and plants, a web of relationships maintains the environment in a balance. If deer start dying off, there are multiple possible explanations. Maybe pollution killed off the grass they ate. Or there were too many deer for the ecosystem to support. Or perhaps a wave of disease killed off the young deer. We need careful investigation to determine causes, and often there are competing explanations for something we observe.

What causes resource shortages?

As the world accumulates more residents, there is a reasonable concern that Earth doesn't have enough resources to go around. But what causes these resource shortages? Are the causes proximate or ultimate? There are three major explanations for the problem.

Too many people

One explanation for resource shortages is that there are simply too many people on Earth and not enough land, water, or food to share around for all of these current and future residents. An excess of people may also affect the natural world. Harvard biologist Dr. E.O. Wilson has said that the combination of consumption and overpopulation could cause half of the world's species to become extinct. The United Nations Environmental Project's Global Environmental Outlook report found that there is simply not enough land on Earth to support the needs of the world's growing population. In other words, too much demand is outpacing the available supply.

Researcher Joel E. Cohen has called this the "fewer forks" explanation, because people who hold this view often say that we need to have "fewer forks" competing for the existing "pie" of Earth's resources. One way to reduce the number of "forks" is to reduce fertility rates and total births so that there is less demand for resources.

Not enough resources

Another explanation for resource shortages is that we are not doing enough to increase the supply of resources to match the increasing demand. People who hold this view say that we have to create what Cohen has called a "bigger pie." That is, we may need to invest in new technologies that will help us get more resources out of what we have now. These new technologies might be agricultural, such as genetically modified crops with improved yields. They might also be environmental, such as factories to remove salt from seawater to increase the availability of fresh water.

Poor distribution of resources

A third explanation for resource shortages is that we have enough resources, but they are poorly distributed due to greed, poor governance, corruption, and poverty. Cohen calls this the "better manners" school of thought. Depending on where you live and the kind of lifestyle you lead, you may consume more or fewer resources than other people on the planet.

ANJIN HEJU
PANAMA

> *Carrying everything and anything*

Huge ships carrying containers full of thousands of different products criss-cross the globe. Is this massive movement of resources from one place to another necessary? In the United States, the food in the average mouthful has traveled more than 1,300 miles, or the distance between Denver, Colorado and San Francisco, California, to reach your plate. This kind of travel uses lots of fuel and emits large quantities of carbon dioxide and other polluting gases.

 The climate change crisis

Many scientists and economists now think that the greatest threat to sustainable development and the ability of Earth to provide for its growing population is climate change. This is a term used to describe significant changes in the normal global weather pattern. Climate changes can involve fluctuations in temperature, changes in levels of precipitation and wind, and the frequency of extreme weather events. All of these changes can have effects on the health and wellbeing of Earth's population. Falls in agricultural production, lessened availability of drinking water, and the spread of diseases to new areas can all be caused by climate change. While climate changes have occurred throughout Earth's history, the global warming caused by rising atmospheric carbon dioxide (CO_2) is believed to be the main culprit in recent increased levels of climate change. Human activity, including industrial pollution, deforestation, and the bi-products of transportation all contribute to this growing crisis. Are governments and individuals doing all they can to reduce climate change and its deadly impact?

The "better manners" explanation suggests that we have enough supply to accommodate demand—we just need to reduce demand so that our existing supplies can be spread around in a more fair way. As one example, consider that a vegetarian diet generally uses fewer resources than a diet that is heavy in meat. This is because it takes more than seven pounds (3.0kg) of grain (as well as water) to produce one pound (0.45kg) of meat.

These three explanations are all about supply and demand. "Fewer forks" and "better manners" both suggest that shortages occur because demand is too high. They say we should reduce the demand for resources so that it is more in line with our available supply. The "bigger pie" explanation says that shortages occur because the supply is too limited, and so we should increase our supply.

> *Sustainable agriculture*

To grow, crops require light, air, and water. They also need nutrients that often come from soil or fertilizer. Every time a farmer harvests crops, they take some of the nutrients with them and away from the soil. Unless those nutrients are replaced, the soil will ultimately become less fertile and crops will not grow as well or at all on that land. Farmers who practice **sustainable agriculture** try to avoid harming the long-term productivity of the land while continuing to raise crops.

The consumption imbalance

Dr. Jared Diamond is a professor of geography at the University of California, Los Angeles. He is the author of the books *Collapse* and *Guns, Germs, and Steel*. As you read his article below, ask yourself which of these explanations about supply and demand he favors. What does he think causes resource shortages? Does he think Earth can support its growing population? What does he think we should do, if anything?

```
What's Your Consumption Factor?
By Jared Diamond

To mathematicians, 32 is an interesting number:
It is 2 raised to the fifth power, 2 times 2
times 2 times 2 times 2. To economists, 32 is even
more special, because it measures the difference
in lifestyles between the first world and the
developing world. The average rates at which people
consume resources like oil and metals, and produce
wastes like plastics and greenhouse gases, are about
32 times higher in North America, Western Europe,
Japan and Australia than they are in the developing
world. That factor of 32 has big consequences.

To understand them, consider our concern with
world population. Today, there are more than 6.5
billion people, and that number may grow to around
9 billion within this half-century. Several decades
ago, many people considered rising population to be
the main challenge facing humanity. Now we realize
that it matters only insofar as people consume
and produce.

If most of the world's 6.5 billion people were in
cold storage and not metabolizing or consuming,
they would create no resource problem. What really
matters is total world consumption, the sum of all
local consumptions, which is the product of local
population times the local per capita consumption
rate.

The estimated one billion people who live in
developed countries have a relative per capita
consumption rate of 32. Most of the world's other
5.5 billion people constitute the developing world,
with relative per capita consumption rates below
32, mostly down toward 1.
```

The population especially of the developing world is growing, and some people remain fixated on this. They note that populations of countries like Kenya are growing rapidly, and they say that's a big problem. Yes, it is a problem for Kenya's more than 30 million people, but it's not a burden on the whole world, because Kenyans consume so little. (Their relative per capita rate is 1.) A real problem for the world is that each of us 300 million Americans consumes as much as 32 Kenyans. With 10 times the population, the United States consumes 320 times more resources than Kenya does...

People who consume little want to enjoy the high-consumption lifestyle. Governments of developing countries make an increase in living standards a primary goal of national policy. And tens of millions of people in the developing world seek the first-world lifestyle on their own, by emigrating, especially to the United States and Western Europe, Japan and Australia. Each such transfer of a person to a high-consumption country raises world consumption rates, even though most immigrants don't succeed immediately in multiplying their consumption by 32.

Among the developing countries that are seeking to increase per capita consumption rates at home, China stands out. It has the world's fastest growing economy, and there are 1.3 billion Chinese, four times the United States population. The world is already running out of resources, and it will do so even sooner if China achieves American-level consumption rates. Already, China is competing with us for oil and metals on world markets.

Per capita consumption rates in China are still about 11 times below ours, but let's suppose they rise to our level. Let's also make things easy by imagining that nothing else happens to increase world consumption—that is, no other country increases its consumption, all national populations (including China's) remain unchanged and immigration ceases. China's catching up alone would roughly double world consumption rates. Oil consumption would increase by 106 percent, for instance, and world metal consumption by 94 percent.

If India as well as China were to catch up, world consumption rates would triple. If the whole developing world were suddenly to catch up, world rates would increase elevenfold. It would be as if the world population ballooned to 72 billion people (retaining present consumption rates).

Some optimists claim that we could support a world with nine billion people. But I haven't met anyone crazy enough to claim that we could support 72 billion. Yet we often promise developing countries that if they will only adopt good policies—for example, institute honest government and a free-market economy—they, too, will be able to enjoy a first-world lifestyle. This promise is impossible, a cruel hoax: we are having difficulty supporting a first-world lifestyle even now for only one billion people.

We Americans may think of China's growing consumption as a problem. But the Chinese are only reaching for the consumption rate we already have. To tell them not to try would be futile.

The only approach that China and other developing countries will accept is to aim to make consumption rates and living standards more equal around the world. But the world doesn't have enough resources to allow for raising China's consumption rates, let alone those of the rest of the world, to our levels. Does this mean we're headed for disaster?

No, we could have a stable outcome in which all countries converge on consumption rates considerably below the current highest levels. Americans might object: there is no way we would sacrifice our living standards for the benefit of people in the rest of the world. Nevertheless, whether we get there willingly or not, we shall soon have lower consumption rates, because our present rates are unsustainable.

Real sacrifice wouldn't be required, however, because living standards are not tightly coupled to consumption rates. Much American consumption is wasteful and contributes little or nothing to quality of life. For example, per capita oil consumption in Western Europe is about half of ours, yet Western Europe's standard of living is higher by any reasonable criterion, including life expectancy, health, infant mortality, access to medical care, financial security after retirement, vacation time, quality of public schools and support for the arts. Ask yourself whether Americans' wasteful use of gasoline contributes positively to any of those measures.

Other aspects of our consumption are wasteful, too. Most of the world's fisheries are still operated non-sustainably, and many have already collapsed or fallen to low yields—even though we know how to manage them in such a way as to preserve the environment and the fish supply. If we were to operate all fisheries sustainably, we could extract fish from the oceans at maximum historical rates and carry on indefinitely.

The same is true of forests: we already know how to log them sustainably, and if we did so worldwide, we could extract enough timber to meet the world's wood and paper needs. Yet most forests are managed non-sustainably, with decreasing yields.

Just as it is certain that within most of our lifetimes we'll be consuming less than we do now, it is also certain that per capita consumption rates in many developing countries will one day be more nearly equal to ours. These are desirable trends, not horrible prospects. In fact, we already know how to encourage the trends; the main thing lacking has been political will.

Fortunately, in the last year there have been encouraging signs. Australia held a recent election in which a large majority of voters reversed the head-in-the-sand political course their government had followed for a decade; the new government immediately supported the Kyoto Protocol on cutting greenhouse gas emissions.

Also in the last year, concern about climate change has increased greatly in the United States. Even in China, vigorous arguments about environmental policy are taking place, and public protests recently halted construction of a huge chemical plant near the center of Xiamen. Hence I am cautiously optimistic. The world has serious consumption problems, but we can solve them if we choose to do so.

[From an article published in the *New York Times* on January 2, 2008]

What do you think?

So, is Dr. Diamond right? Could we reduce our consumption of resources if we wanted to? Could we reduce it enough to sustain Earth's growing population?

One way to measure resource use is by looking at your ecological footprint. Your ecological footprint is an estimate of your personal use of natural resources, based on an estimate of the amount of land and sea necessary to regenerate the resources you use. Normally, your ecological footprint is calculated in terms of "global hectares," a standardized unit of land area. For example, in the United States, the average ecological footprint is 9.6 global hectares per person, while in the United Kingdom it is 5.45. Researchers William Rees and Mathis Wackernagel, who invented the concept of the ecological footprint, estimate that for **sustainability**, the average footprint for all people on Earth should be 1.8. This is because, with 6 billion people on Earth, there exists only 1.8 global hectares each of productive land and sea.

There are several methods on Internet sites you can use to calculate your ecological footprint. These calculators take into account whether you walk, drive, or take the bus. They consider how much you recycle, and what kind of food you eat. Finding out your ecological footprint might surprise you, even if you think you do not use many resources at all.

✔ Ecological Debt Day

Every year, the Global Footprint Network marks Ecological Debt Day, the day during the course of the year when Earth's population begins living beyond its means. The timing of this day is based on the global ecological footprint, compared with the actual resources available on Earth. As human consumption increases, the day is moved earlier and earlier. In 2007, Ecological Debt Day was October 6.

According to the Global Footprint Network, "On Ecological Debt Day, we go into global overshoot for a given year and begin contributing to our global ecological debt, which has been accumulating since we first went into overshoot in the 1980s."

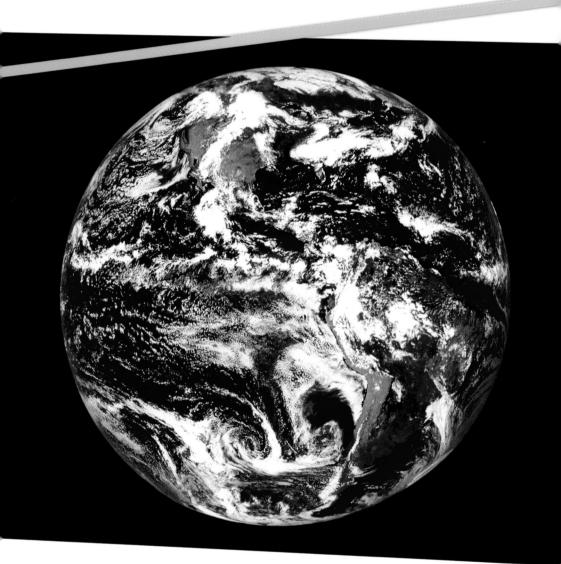

> *Spaceship Earth*

Earth is a closed ecosystem. Other than the occasional asteroid and rays from the Sun, very little comes in or out. This means that changes in one area usually affect other areas, and can have lasting consequences. Whatever the effects of human population increases, they are sure to be around for a long time to come.

How Far Will Earth Stretch?

Easter Island is an isolated dot of land in the Pacific Ocean, thousands of miles away from the next nearest inhabited land. When the first humans arrived there, they found a lush environment with trees and an ample supply of food. In 1722, Dutch explorer Jacob Roggeveen visited the island and observed a thriving community of several thousand people, but by then the island had been stripped of all of its trees. By 1877, little more than 100 people were left on the island. Explanations for this population crash vary, but most people agree that as the island was depleted of its resources, it could no longer sustain its previous population levels.

Clearly, our planet is a vastly more complex ecosystem than tiny, isolated Easter Island. Most people do not believe that a population crash of this magnitude would happen on Earth. But, like the people of Easter Island, we are putting a serious strain on the capacity of Earth and on its resources.

In this chapter, you need to think about four major areas of strain on our planet. These areas of strain correspond to the four basic human needs: shelter, air, food, and water.

The shelter shortage

A growing population needs somewhere to live. This means that Earth's available land space is increasingly stretched and stressed, as more people try to inhabit the same space. Those who don't move to cities often move to previously uninhabited areas to try and carve out a new living space. This often means clearing out forested land to grow crops. In tropical areas like Brazil, this trend has resulted in widespread deforestation. The problem with clearing the rain forest is that the soil there tends to have low levels of nutrients and be easily depleted. This means that farmers trying to grow crops in the rain forest have to continually clear more and more land to make a living. Since 1990, the world has lost about 502,000 square miles (1.3 million square kilometers) of forest. Once cleared, forests—especially rain forests and "old growth" forests—rarely return unless there is a serious effort made to regenerate them.

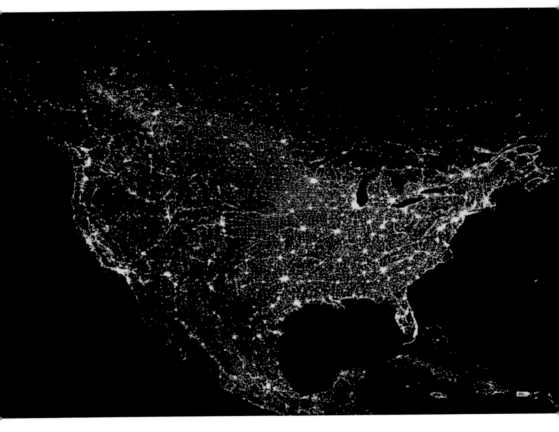

> *The light at night*

As Earth's population grows, more people move to cities in search of work and a higher standard of living. These people often find themselves living in slums or other substandard housing without access to sanitary living conditions. The lights at night on this U.S. satellite photo show the concentrations of people. Large cities show up as bigger white blobs.

But forests are important for sustaining human life as well as the life of other animals. Forests are home to half of the species on Earth, and also act as important reservoirs for carbon dioxide. Because trees take in carbon dioxide and "exhale" oxygen, they help Earth recycle its air and slow the process of global warming.

Population growth also speeds up the process of erosion. Erosion is a natural process that happens when the top layers of land are stripped away. The expansion of human population contributes to erosion as people move into previously uncultivated areas and fail to use sustainable agriculture.

But better land use policies can reduce the impact that population growth has on the environment. In Brazil, the Amazon Regional Protected Area Program protects and manages more than 12 percent of the Brazilian Amazon. In other countries, strict prosecution of illegal logging in forests has reduced deforestation while allowing countries to cut trees in a sustainable manner that increases funds for government projects. And sustainable agriculture techniques can substantially reduce erosion. But more is needed to encourage **sustainable development** through effective land use policies. In many places corruption and lack of political will to improve things contribute to shelter problems.

Slums: a global problem

"Slums are the stage to the most acute scenarios of urban poverty, physical and environmental deprivation. Approximately one-third of the urban population globally live in these conditions. Typical slums in developing countries are unplanned informal settlements where access to services is minimal to non-existent and where overcrowding is the norm. Slum conditions result in placing residents at a higher risk of disease, mortality and misfortune. 94% of the world's slum dwellers live in developing regions, which are the regions experiencing the most rapid growth in urban populations and with the least capacity to accommodate this growth. Where available, trend data indicate that this problem is worsening. UN-HABITAT estimates that in 2001 there were 924 million slum dwellers in the world and that without significant intervention to improve access to water, sanitation, secure tenure and adequate housing this number could grow to 1.5 billion by 2020."

From a paper given by Willem de Vries, SCORUS, Potsdam, 2003:
http://busmgt.ulst.ac.uk/scorus/potsdam/013.pdf

The air we breathe

Along with food and water, all people need air—clean air—to survive. But Earth's growing population is putting more pollution into the atmosphere than ever before. This pollution takes many forms. The most common are sulfur dioxide, ozone, and particulate matter found in **smog**. Since more than half Earth's residents live in cities, and smog is primarily an urban problem, this means that billions of people are exposed to air pollution on a regular basis. Some of this pollution contains dangerous heavy metals, such as lead, which can cause severe brain damage and even death. Although many countries have passed laws removing lead from gasoline, the majority of the world still uses leaded gasoline.

A growing population needs fuel. And in most of the world, that fuel is a mix of coal and what's called **biomass**: living or dead biological material. These fuels, when burned, produce high concentrations of the gases commonly

> *The issue of air pollution*

Air pollution has serious consequences. The American Association for the Advancement of Science estimates that in China's largest cities, smog causes 50,000 deaths every year and 40,000 cases of chronic bronchitis. Because smog has a high acid content, it can cause "acid rain," a condition where the pollutants in the smog are carried down in rainfall, contaminating water and soil.

associated with global warming. A consensus of scientists believes that human activity contributes to global warming. It makes sense, therefore, that more human activity will make more of a contribution to global warming. The World Health Organization (WHO) warns:

"More than half of the world's population rely on dung, wood, crop waste or coal to meet their most basic energy needs. Cooking and heating with such solid fuels on open fires or stoves without chimneys leads to indoor air pollution. This indoor smoke contains a range of health-damaging pollutants including small soot or dust particles that are able to penetrate deep into the lungs. In poorly ventilated dwellings, indoor smoke can exceed acceptable levels for small particles in outdoor air 100-fold. Exposure is particularly high among women and children, who spend the most time near the domestic hearth. Every year, indoor air pollution is responsible for the death of 1.6 million people—that's one death every 20 seconds. According to the 2004 assessment of the International Energy Agency, the number of people relying on biomass fuels such as wood, dung, and agricultural residues for cooking and heating will continue to rise. In sub-Saharan Africa, the reliance on biomass fuels appears to be growing as a result of population growth and the unavailability of, or increases in the price of, alternatives such as kerosene and liquid petroleum gas."

[From the WHO website http://www.who.int/mediacentre/factsheets/fs292/en/index.html]

Threats from climate change

The world's climate is changing quickly. A recent report by the United Nations Intergovernmental Panel on Climate Change concluded that if the world does not immediately reduce its emissions of greenhouse gases, we will suffer from a global climate crisis that could reduce crop yields in Africa by as much as 50 percent and cause sea level increases that would submerge some island states and major coastal cities.

Population growth contributes to rather than causes air pollution and global warming. It also complicates the question of how to solve these pressing problems. While many countries have committed to reducing their greenhouse gas emissions, it is not clear whether these reductions will be enough to make up for the increases in other parts of the world.

> *Will the fish be gone?*
> Nineteen percent of the world's protein supply comes from the oceans. But fish supplies are being reduced at an alarming rate due to overfishing and increased demand. In 2006, a study published in the journal *Science* found that one-third of fishing stocks have collapsed and that it is possible, if current trends continue, that all global fish stocks will collapse within 50 years.

Global hunger

The world is hungry. The World Health Organization estimates that in any given year, one-third of the world is starving, one-third is underfed, and one third is well fed. Six million children under the age of five die every year because of hunger, and more than 840 million people are malnourished. Most malnutrition occurs in the world's poorest countries. Earth's newest residents are likely to arrive in countries where there is barely enough food to feed the people who already live there, and where there is little planning for new arrivals. As the population grows, hunger is likely to become a more serious issue.

This is not necessarily because population growth increases hunger. On the contrary, in theory the world produces more than enough food to feed everyone. A 2002 report by the United Nations' Food and Agriculture Organization calculated that world agriculture produces 17 percent more calories than it did 30 years ago, despite a 70 percent population increase. The major issue is poverty. Poor people cannot buy land to grow their own food, neither do they have money to buy food.

Many countries do not even produce enough food to feed their citizens. We say that these countries are "net importers" of food, which means that they import more food than they export. This is a dangerous situation to be in, as countries that import food are not self-sufficient, and are vulnerable to changes in the price of food over time.

With regard to the supply of food, there may be enough to go around, but existing distribution systems are clearly not working to get food to the neediest people. Supply can still be increased with better agricultural practices, such as sustainable agriculture and the removal of **agricultural subsidies** in the developed world. More needs to be done to increase the use of better practices—especially in poor nations. However, reduction of consumption in the developed world might also go a long way toward freeing up food supplies for developing areas.

Enough food to go around

There are those who think that there is definitely enough food to feed the world. This excerpt is from testimony given by Sheldon Richman, a Senior Editor at the Cato Institute:

"Food is abundant. Since 1948, according to the UN Food and Agriculture Organization and the U.S. Department of Agriculture, annual world food production has outpaced the increase in population. Today, per capita production and per-acre yields are at all-time highs. Prices of agricultural products have been falling for over 100 years. The average inflation-adjusted price of those products, indexed to wages, fell by more than 74 percent between 1950 and 1990. While Lester Brown of the Worldwatch Institute and the noted butterfly expert Paul Ehrlich predict higher food prices and increasing scarcity, food is becoming cheaper and more plentiful. That good news is due largely to technological advances (the "green revolution") that have provided better seeds, fertilizers, pesticides, and methods of farming. The only obstacles to agricultural progress are the impediments created by governments. Imagine what the world would be like today if the fertile farmland of the former Soviet Union or China or India had been in productive private hands operating in free markets for the past several decades. Since permitting market incentives in agriculture, India has become a net food exporter and agricultural production in China has boomed."

[From Sheldon Richman online at http://www.cato.org/ttestimony/ct-ps720.html]

Drying up

Most people in wealthier nations aren't used to thinking of water as a scarce commodity. After all, you probably have access to clean water at any tap in your house. But more than two billion people lack access to drinkable, or potable, water and sanitation.

Obviously, people need water to live. This means that without access to clean water, people will still drink whatever water is available. And all too often, that water is infected with parasites and diseases that can cause death. According to the World Health Organization, at any given time up to one half of humanity is affected by the major diseases carried by dirty water and poor sanitation. These diseases, which include diarrhea, schistosomiasis, trachoma, and infestation with ascaris, guinea worm, or hookworm, kill millions of people every year.

> *Dirty water = thirsty people*

Earth's growing population isn't doing a good job of keeping its water supplies clean. With more mouths to feed, farmers are under increasing pressure to use fertilizers that pollute groundwater, rivers, and coastal ecosystems. More people means more trash needing disposal. Many of the world's cities still dump raw sewage into their waters, leaving Earth's scarce fresh water supplies even worse off.

Trashing the ocean

All around the world, the oceans and seas have been used as "bottomless" garbage containers. Author Susan Casey gives some gruesome details:

"At the same time, all over the globe, there are signs that plastic pollution is doing more than blighting the scenery; it is also making its way into the food chain. Some of the most obvious victims are the dead seabirds that have been washing ashore in startling numbers, their bodies packed with plastic: things like bottle caps, cigarette lighters, tampon applicators, and colored scraps that, to a foraging bird, resemble baitfish. (One animal dissected by Dutch researchers contained 1,603 pieces of plastic.) And the birds aren't alone. All sea creatures are threatened by floating plastic, from whales down to zooplankton. There's a basic moral horror in seeing the pictures: a sea turtle with a plastic band strangling its shell into an hourglass shape; a humpback towing plastic nets that cut into its flesh and make it impossible for the animal to hunt. More than a million seabirds, 100,000 marine mammals, and countless fish die in the North Pacific each year, either from mistakenly eating this junk or from being ensnared in it and drowning."

[This excerpt is from the article "Plastic Ocean," by Susan Casey, published in Best Life magazine on February 20, 2007. http://www.bestlifeonline.com/cms/publish/travel-leisure/Our_oceans_are_turning_into_plastic_are_we.shtml]

Even when populations have access to clean water, it may simply not be enough. The World Bank reports that global demand for water is doubling every 21 years—faster even than the rate of population growth. Once climate change is factored in, with some regions experiencing intensive droughts, it is clear that humanity faces some tough choices about its water use.

Unfortunately, some countries may choose to go to war to protect their water supplies. Since rivers cross borders and are essential to sustain life, they are part of tense negotiations and even armed conflicts.

But there are some solutions to the coming water crunch. Promising new technologies, such as desalinization plants that extract salt from seawater, could produce abundant fresh water. Countries could also work to dramatically reduce their water use in manufacturing, industry, and personal consumption. But there is no denying the impact population growth will have on our ability to make sure every person has access to clean, fresh, water.

> *Is the world one massive, smelly traffic jam?*

There are 500 million cars on the road right now, producing ten trillion cubic meters of exhaust fumes every year. These fumes contain about 15 percent of global carbon dioxide and 90 percent of carbon monoxide emissions. People with cars are unlikely to want to give them up and those living in growing economies, such as China and India, also want cars. This is part of the reason that global car ownership is expected to double by 2030.

What Should We Do?

Too small a pie? Too many forks? Bad manners? Or is poverty and bad government at the root of this problem? Whatever the cause, it's clear that it will be difficult at best for Earth to sustain its growing population. This is especially true if population continues to increase, consumption levels remain high, and we fail to increase our available resources to meet basic human needs.

Earlier in the book, you read about three major explanations for resource shortages. In this chapter, you'll look at solutions offered from those three perspectives to consider what our response to growing population and resource shortages should be.

The stakes are high. Billions of lives and the quality of life for everyone on Earth are at risk, and the decisions we make in the next few decades will be critical. What is done now will determine the quality of life, and even the survival of life for future generations.

Controlling population growth

One popular solution to the resource crunch and global population growth is simply to reduce the number of people on Earth, usually by slowing the rate of growth. Family planning policies try to reduce the birthrate by educating people about reproductive options. In most cases, this includes education about abstaining from sex until marriage, contraception methods, and effective parenting practices. In general, family planning programs, when used, are highly effective at reducing fertility and population growth. But family planning is still controversial. In some parts of the world with large Catholic populations, such as South America, there are religious objections to contraception. In China, official family planning policy has been to limit each couple to only one child. And in some parts of the world, family planning programs have been used to sterilize women without their permission—although this practice has dropped off in recent years.

There are many challenges facing family planning programs. The United Nations estimates that if the world is to reach a stable population level, 75 percent of all couples in the world must use contraception. In some countries, official policy is moving in the opposite direction. Russia has recently offered financial incentives to women who have multiple children in an effort to increase that country's population. Low fertility rates in countries like Japan and Germany have caused some to worry about those nations' financial futures. Fewer young people means a smaller number of workers, a shrinking number of taxpayers, and a larger proportion of elderly people (as depicted in the "Population Pyramids" on page 17).

Reducing consumption

Another approach is consumption reduction. As you already know, there are not enough resources to go around at current levels of consumption. Many people say that instead of telling people in poor countries to have fewer children, residents of rich countries should mind their own business first by reducing their consumption levels. Whether you agree with this point of view or not, it is hard to deny a general need for consumption reduction. As an individual, you can decrease your consumption in basic ways like reducing automobile travel, recycling, reusing products, and being conscious of your dietary choices. Eating locally produced and in-season foods, or even consuming a mostly vegetarian diet, can reduce your ecological footprint by up to 10 percent.

Other steps to reduce consumption are best accomplished at a larger level. For example, societies could invest heavily in the use of renewable or "clean" energy sources, like solar power and nuclear power. These would reduce coal and oil consumption while reducing pollution.

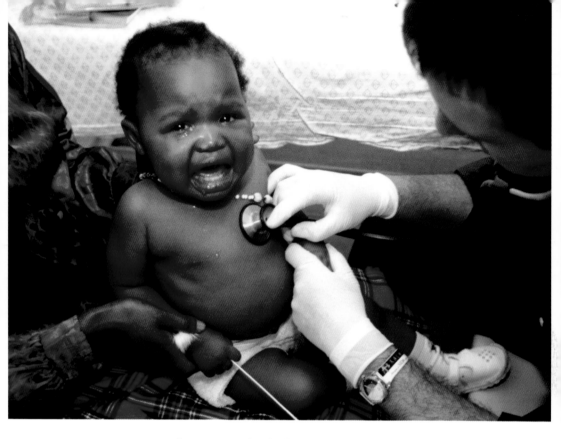

> *Strategies to reduce birthrates*

One popular solution to the world's population growth is expanded family planning, which involves a combination of birth control, poverty reduction, and education. In many parts of the world, infant mortality is so high that families have many children to try and ensure that some will survive to adulthood. Strategies to reduce infant mortality and increase health care can be part of a larger effort to reduce birthrates.

Is redistribution the way out?

Resources and income could also be redistributed, or channeled from those who are rich to those who are poor, so that consumption patterns shift to accommodate emerging needs. One way to do this would be to use tax policy to increase the price of luxury goods, goods that use scarce resources, or products that have environmental consequences. These kinds of taxes generally force people to reduce their consumption. A global carbon tax has also been suggested. These policies are controversial, however. Many people believe that governments should not get involved in setting the price of goods and services, and that free markets will work better to solve environmental problems without government intervention.

> *Will new technologies help?*

New technologies, such as genetically modified crops, promise to increase yields while allowing plants to grow in more difficult environments with minimal water and fertilizer. These new agricultural technologies could help to sustain the world's growing population, but carry their own risks. Some say that reliance on genetically modified foods increases plant viruses that can destroy whole crops, leading to widespread hunger.

Making the pie bigger

Since 1798 when Thomas Malthus wrote his gloomy book, *Essay on the Principle of Population*, plenty of predictions about an apocalypse caused by population growth have proven to be wrong. The world's population has continued to increase, despite predictions of impending global famines. The price of natural resources, like coal and trees, remains low and generally affordable. One of the reasons for this is that humans are incredibly resourceful and constantly developing new technologies to find and make the most of available resources. These new technologies hold a lot of promise for reducing the impact of the resource crunch and helping Earth sustain its growing population.

In the twentieth century, the "Green Revolution" in agriculture mixed traditional agricultural techniques with new technologies and high-yield crops in countries such as India. It is widely credited with allowing food production to keep up with population growth, saving many millions of lives. But it was not without costs. The Green Revolution encouraged the development of **monocultures** and use of expensive seed varieties from Western countries. Many poor countries produced more food, but their residents could not afford to eat it.

Other new technologies, like water desalinization, improved public transportation, and even advances that we can't now imagine are likely to help reduce the impact of population growth and high levels of consumption. Human inventiveness has a good track record when faced with difficult situations and high demand.

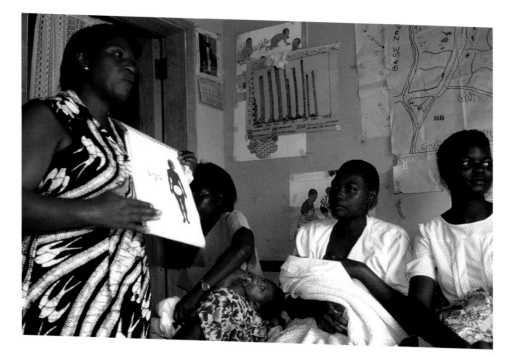

> *Are women the answer?*

One of the most reliable ways to reduce a population's growth rate is to educate and raise the social status of women. This may be because women use their knowledge to improve home living conditions, decreasing infant mortality. It may be because educated women are more likely to use contraception. It may be that educated women are more likely to seek careers and status outside of the home, reducing the number of children they bear. Whatever the reason, multiple studies have supported women's education as a way to reduce population growth.

> *Get involved*

Population growth and resource consumption are some
of the most important issues facing your generation and
generations to come. Understanding the related issues
and having informed opinions about them is essential to
making decisions in your own life, as well as in larger
social and political arenas.

What Do You Think?

The world's population is growing. There's little debate about that. The real question, as the title of this book indicates, is whether Earth can support this population. How you answer this question depends on the evidence and how it is interpreted. It might be that the current course of action is not a good one. But that doesn't mean Earth can't support its population. But it might be that it can't do so without a change of course.

What will that change of course look like? It depends on what you think the cause or causes of resource shortages are, and how you think we should address those causes. This book contains a lot of information, and has barely scratched the surface of a problem that threatens to affect the lives of all people around the world.

As you work to form your own opinion, it will be useful to do additional research and think critically about the issues to decide what you think about this extremely important question: Can Earth support its growing population?

Population: a global issue

The world's population is increasing. Birth rates continue to increase at about one percent a year while death rates are declining. This means that there are more people on Earth than at any time in human history. And even though growth rates are declining, population continues to increase due to momentum created by the total size of our population. This means that there is an increasing possibility of resource shortages. These shortages affect all areas of life, including access to food, water, fuel, shelter, and clean air.

However, these shortages are not necessarily caused by population increases. They might be caused by over consumption or by a lack of new technologies to increase resources. As Jared Diamond commented on pages 25-28, resource shortages may be inevitable even if population growth stops. It may be unfair or even dangerous to blame population growth for resource shortages, distracting us from the real solutions.

Has your opinion changed?

So what do you think? What causes resource shortages? Are population increases the problem? What about distribution of resources? Or the development of new technologies? And what should we do about our existing problems? Should we pursue family planning programs? Should we reduce our consumption? Are these solutions realistic? Will they work in time? It is up to you to consider these and other questions as you debate the central issue of this book.

How to debate

There are three important parts of a debate in any format. First, all participants must be able to make arguments to defend their side. Remember that arguments should have three parts: assertion, reasoning, and evidence (**A–R–E**). Second, participants should make sure that they respond to opposing arguments. It's not enough just to make an argument for your side; you also have to answer what the other side says. This is called refutation. Third, it is important to take notes during any debate or discussion. This will allow you to track arguments as they're made, prepare to respond to the other side, and organize your ideas for upcoming speeches.

Two-sided debate

One side makes a case for the topic. The other side argues against the case. The side arguing for the topic is called the proposition or affirmative; the other side is called the opposition or negative. Each speaker on a side delivers a speech. The teams alternate speakers. The proposition team, which must prove that the topic is more likely to be true, speaks first and last. The opening proposition speaker makes a case. The first opposition speaker refutes the case. Second speakers continue with their team's points and refute new points from the other side. The final speeches are summaries of the best arguments for a team and the best refutation against the major points of the other side. With six students, you would have the following format and speaker times:

First speaker, proposition – 5 minutes
First speaker, opposition – 5 minutes
Second speaker, proposition – 5 minutes
Second speaker, opposition – 5 minutes
Third speaker, opposition – 3 minutes
Third speaker, proposition – 3 minutes

It is possible to add question and comment time by the opposing side or a class or audience during, in between, or after speeches.

> *Our battered planet*

Is population growth too much for Earth to take? Or can we take steps to reduce the impact, preserving the quality of life for billions of people? Only time will tell, but the actions of people in your generation will determine the outcome through personal choices and policy reform.

✔ Speaking your mind

Many people are intimidated by the idea of delivering a speech in class or in public. It's true that public speaking can be hard, but it should be no more difficult than reading a book or writing an essay. It takes preparation and practice. A few key steps can make the difference between an uninspired speech and a great one.

✔ **Prepare**. Research your topic thoroughly. Have plenty of facts and arguments to support your position. Make sure your evidence is credible and your reasoning is sound.

✔ **Organize**. Good speeches are organized, and the best way to start is by writing an outline. Your speech should have a thesis statement and supporting points. Your supporting points will be especially effective if organized using the A–R–E method.

✔ **Practice**. You don't need to memorize your speech, but it is very important to practice. Try to speak from minimal notes, reducing your outline to a few points. This way you won't be reading from a script and boring your audience.

✔ **Relax**. When you're delivering your speech, try to relax and take deep breaths. It's okay to depart from your script a little bit, or even make a joke. This doesn't mean you should be unprofessional, but audiences do respond well to speakers who seem friendly.

✔ **Afterwards**. After your speech, it's a good idea to answer questions from the audience, if appropriate. This gives you a chance to clear up any lingering misconceptions or misunderstandings, as well as to share information with the audience.

Discussion

A group of students participates in a panel discussion on an issue. Students speak for themselves and may agree or disagree with the opinions of others on the panel. The discussion is designed to inform an audience. There is an overall time limit, for example, 30 minutes, for the entire discussion. You can use a moderator to ask questions and keep the discussion moving. A panel discussion is an opportunity to use conversation in a way that presents and challenges ideas. Audience questions may be added after the discussion.

Open forum

This is an effective format for a class or large group. A single moderator leads an open discussion on a range of topics. Members of the audience may present new ideas, add to the presentations from others, or refute any issue. Like brainstorming, this format quickly gets a variety of ideas into a discussion.

> *Join the debate*

Make sure, when you debate, that you make complete arguments and take care to refute your opponent's arguments. It is possible to have an individual or group judge a debate, voting on the outcome. For larger discussions, it is possible to ask an audience which person did the best job and why.

Now that you have researched and debated the issue, are your feelings and opinions the same? Can Earth support its growing population? What do you think?

Find Out More

Books

- Brown, C, R. Lester and G. Gardner. *Beyond Malthus: Nineteen Dimensions of the Population Challenge*. New York: W.W. Norton, 1999.

- David, L. and C. Gordon. *The Down-to-Earth Guide to Global Warming*. New York: Scholastic, 2007.

- Leisinger, Klaus M. *Six Billion and Counting : Population Growth and Food Security in the 21st Century*. Washington, D.C.: International Food Policy Research Institute, 2002.

- Malthus, Thomas R. *An Essay on the Principle of Population* (Norton Critical Editions), ed. Philip Appleman. 2nd ed. New York: W.W. Norton, 2003.

- Mason, Paul. *Planet Under Pressure: Population*. Chicago: Raintree, 2006.

- Stiglitz, Joseph. *Making Globalization Work*. New York: W. W. Norton, 2006.

Websites

- **Global Footprint Network**
  http://www.footprintnetwork.org/index.php
  Contains helpful information about measuring and reducing ecological footprints.

- **National Geographic Eye in the Sky: Overpopulation**
  http://www.nationalgeographic.com/eye/overpopulation/overpopulation.html
  National Geographic photographs and video clips show evidence of overpopulation on Earth and methods to help control it.

- **Population Reference Bureau**
  http://www.prb.org/Home.aspx
  The website of this non-partisan organization collects lots of useful information about global population issues.

◆ The World Bank

http://www.worldbank.org/
The website of the World Bank collects economic and social information on countries all over the world.

◆ World Population Clock

http://www.census.gov/ipc/www/popclockworld.html
From the U.S. Census, this website tracks world population in real time.

Movies

◆ *A. I. Artificial Intelligence* (2001)

◆ *The Day After Tomorrow* (2004)

◆ *Logan's Run* (1976)

Debate resources

◆ Shuster, Kate, and John Meany.*Speak Out! Debate and Public Speaking in the Middle Grades*. New York: IDEA Press, 2005.

◆ Middle School Public Debate Program
www.middleschooldebate.com
Comprehensive debate instruction for the classroom and competitive contests.

◆ Guidelines for Deliberation and Discussion
http://www.choices.edu/deliberation.cfm
Some helpful tips for having productive discussions, from the *Choices Program* at Brown University.

Glossary

agricultural subsidies money paid to farmers for producing certain crops or not using certain land

aquifer underground geological formation that holds water

average also known as the mean, is the sum of a series of numbers divided by the number of items in that series

biomass living or dead biological material, often used for fuel

carrying capacity population size that an ecosystem can support given its available resources including food, shelter, and water

consumption use of goods and services

deforestation removal of trees from land, converting previously forested land to land used for other purposes

demography science of studying populations using statistics

demographic transition something that happens in industrialized countries. It is a change from high birth rates and high death rates to low birth rates and low death rates.

ecosystem specific interaction of plants, animals, and climate

epidemic widespread outbreak of an infectious disease

exponential growth growth rate that gets bigger as the size of a population increases

family planning schemes to reduce birthrates by educating people about reproductive options. In most cases, this includes education about abstaining from sex until marriage, contraception methods, and effective parenting.

fertility physical ability to have children

fertility rate number of children born to a population, normally per year

globalization global relationship between cultures that is made possible through the movement of people, goods, and ideas

mean	also known as the average, is the sum of a series of numbers divided by the number of items in that series
median	middle number in a list of numbers arranged from highest to lowest. If there is an even number of items in the list, the median is the average of the two middle numbers.
mode	number that occurs most frequently in a list of numbers
monocultures	use of land to grow only one type of crop
mortality rate	number of people who die in a particular population, normally per year
proximate cause	"trigger" for an event, or the initial act that caused it
renewable resource	resource replenished continually through natural processes
replacement fertility rate	population producing 2.1 children per adult
resource	commodity, usually a physical thing
smog	dust, smoke, or chemical fumes that pollute the air and create hazy, unhealthy conditions
standard of living	level and amount of goods and services that are available to people, and how those goods and services are shared within a population
sustainability	process or state of affairs that can be maintained indefinitely
sustainable agriculture	agricultural practices that can be used without depleting the soil or causing other harmful effects, such as erosion
sustainable development	economic and physical expansion that meets human needs while maintaining balance with the natural world
ultimate cause	underlying, fundamental, or "root" cause of an event

Index